ASTRO-GALAXY

(LOVE UR STAR)

PADMA MANI

B.Com, MBA, PGDBA, PGDA, DOA

Edition - 29 Jan 2021

CONTENTS

ACKNOWLEDGEMENTS

I dedicate this book to my Late Father-in-Law Mr. K. Sambandam, the man, who supported and guided me for few years. He had a strong belief on Stars and their influence on individuals. He keeps telling me, that you have to know your star and do the remedies accordingly, so you can reduce the trouble. He had an attitude of checking the calendar everyday, before he steps out of home.

When I look into his words, every individual born on earth has a zodiac sign. Zodiac sign reflects the individual's personality, attitude, motivation and their identity.

His thoughts and belief, inspired me to do further study, research, discuss and analyze to know every detail about astrology to know about facts and their remedies.

INTRODUCTION

Astrology is a study of Stars & Planets around the earth.
There are infinite stars around the galaxy, but we have only 27 stars named and reflects on indiviudals. Why?

27 Stars positioned and moving around the earth, which are 400 light years away from earth.

There is a belief, that Moon has 27 wives and they are 27 stars. 27 stars have 4 houses in which the particular star will hide in particular house for moon to find his wife (little romantic). Moon searches for his wife in these 4 houses (paadham/phase) and resides with each star a day to satisfy them. Based on the moon's movement and residing in each star, ancient people calculated time and the connecting star for new born.

How is number 9 important?
Numbers - 9 (0 not to be included)
Planets - 9
Gem Stones - 9
Stars - 9 (27 = 2+7=9)
4 Houses of Stars - 9 (27 x 4 = 108, 1+0+8=9)
9 can be converted as 6 (both directions can be seen either as 9 or 6)
96 - referred to be a partial masculine and feminine (this is how trans-genders are referred).

9 has been considered as a very powerful and aspicious numbers, both in astrology & numerology.

I have tried to simplify the Astrology, in easy terms to understand and get benefited.

ASTRO PLANETS

Here we will see about 9 planets that are connected with calendar days and their astrological names

PLANET	DAY	ASTRO TERM
SUN	SUNDAY	SURIYAN
MOON	MONDAY	CHANDIRAN
MARS	TUESDAY	SEVVAI
MERCURY	WEDNESDAY	PUDHAN
JUPITER	THURSDAY	GURU
VENUS	FRIDAY	SUKIRAN
SATURN	SATURDAY	SANI
RAAGU	TUESDAY	RAAGU
KETHU	SATURDAY	KETHU

PLANETS & THEIR GENDER

We know that there are 9 planets, but how do we know which gender they belong too. Its basic knowledge we need to know which gender our planet belongs, that governs us.

PLANET	ASTRO TERM	GENDER
SUN	SURIYAN	MALE
MOON	CHANDIRAN	FEMALE
MARS	SEVVAI	MALE
MERCURY	PUDHAN	TRANSGENDER
JUPITER	GURU	MALE
VENUS	SUKIRAN	FEMALE
SATURN	SANI	TRANSGENDER
RAAGU	RAAGU	FEMALE
KETHU	KETHU	TRANSGENDER

GEM STONES

There are precious 9 gem stones which is connected to our stars & planets.

Gem stones are used for their positive vibes and ability to influence the situation for optimal output. It is believed that gem stones can change the individual's life, health, wealth and more.

1. CORAL (PAVAZHAM)
2. PEARL (MUTHU)
3. HESSONITE (KOMEDHAGHAM)
4. EMERALD (MARAGATHAM)
5. DIAMOND (VAIRAM)
6. SAPPHIRE (NEELAM)
7. TOPAZ (PUSHPARAGAM)
8. RUBY (MAANICKAM)
9. CAT'S EYE (VAIDURYIAM)

ZODIAC SIGNS

There are 12 Zodiac signs which are connected to the planets and their stars. 4 stars and their 4 houses are divided to each Zodiac which connects the planets.

Moon sign is referred by Time, Date, Month & Year of an individual.

Sun Sign is referred by Date & Month of an individual.

SUN Sign & MOON Sign

1. ARIES -- MESHAM
2. TAURUS -- RISHABAM
3. GEMINI -- MITHUNAM
4. CANCER -- KADAGAM
5. LEO -- SIMHAM
6. VIRGO -- KAANI
7. LIBRA -- THULAM
8. SCORPIO -- VIRUCHUGAM
9. SAGITTARIUS -- DHANUSU
10. CAPRICON -- MAGARAM
11. AQUARIUS -- KUMBAM
12. PISCES -- MEENAM

ZODIAC SIGNS & THEIR GENDER

Every Zodiac has its own gender identity which impacts the individual's mind & their thoughts

1. ARIES / MESHAM -- MALE
2. TAURUS / RISHABAM -- FEMALE
3. GEMINI / MITHUNAM -- TRANSGENDER
4. CANCER / KADAGAM -- FEMALE
5. LEO / SIMHAM -- MALE

6. VIRGO / KAANI -- FEMALE
7. LIBRA -- THULAM -- MALE
8. SCORPIO -- VIRUCHUGAM -- FEMALE
9. SAGITTARIUS / DHANUSU -- TRANSGENDER
10. CAPRICON / MAGARAM -- TRANSGENDER
11. AQUARIUS / KUMBAM -- MALE
12. PISCES / MEENAM -- FEMALE

ZODIAC & THEIR PLANETS

Every Zodiac is been guided by a planet. Every planet has its own qualities.

1. ARIES / MESHAM -- MARS
2. TAURUS / RISHABAM -- VENUS
3. GEMINI / MITHUNAM -- MERCURY
4. CANCER / KADAGAM -- MOON
5. LEO / SIMHAM -- SUN
6. VIRGO / KAANI -- MERCURY
7. LIBRA -- THULAM -- VENUS
8. SCORPIO -- VIRUCHUGAM -- MARS
9. SAGITTARIUS / DHANUSU -- JUPITER
10. CAPRICON / MAGARAM -- SATURN
11. AQUARIUS / KUMBAM -- SATURN
12. PISCES / MEENAM -- JUPITER

ZODIAC SIGNS & SYMBOLS

In Stone ages, Symbols are been used to refer Zodiac Signs. They use to put tatoo of the symbol on new borns to recognize their groups (Planet) and their talents.

Later by astrological scientists, names were identified and used in generations.

Even now, we can see people put tatoo of their zodiac symbols on their body.

Zodiac Signs & Symbols

1. ARIES -- MESHAM -- The Ram
2. TAURUS -- RISHABAM -- The Bull
3. GEMINI -- MITHUNAM -- The Twins
4. CANCER -- KADAGAM -- The Crab
5. LEO -- SIMHAM -- The Lion
6. VIRGO -- KAANI -- The Virgin
7. LIBRA -- THULAM -- The Balance
8. SCORPIO -- VIRUCHUGAM -- The Scorpion
9. SAGITTARIUS -- DHANUSU -- The Archer
10. CAPRICON -- MAGARAM -- The Sea-sGoat
11. AQUARIUS -- KUMBAM -- The WaterBearer
12. PISCES -- MEENAM-- The Fishes

SUN SIGNS & CALENDAR

Sun Sign is referred by Date & Month of an individual.
Sun sign has been used majorily by the western cultured people.

Sun Sign & Calendar

1. ARIES -- Mar 21–Apr 19
2. TAURUS -- Apr 20–May 20
3. GEMINI -- May 21–Jun 21
4. CANCER -- Jun 22–Jul 22
5. LEO -- Jul 23–Aug 22
6. VIRGO -- Aug 23–Sep 22
7. LIBRA -- Sep 23–Oct 23
8. SCORPIO -- Oct 24–Nov 21
9. SAGITTARIUS -- Nov 22–Dec 21
10. CAPRICON -- Dec 22–Jan 19
11. AQUARIUS -- Jan 20–Feb 18
12. PISCES -- Feb 19–Mar 20

Sun sign shows your personality, but it would be influnced by another zodiac sign and this is where an individual needs to know their Moon Sign in additional.
Both Sun and Moon signs will help us to have a deepest understanding and bonding of our emotions, which are inter-connected between Sun and Moon.

ZODIAC & ELEMENTS

There are 4 Elements which will be connected to each of our Zodiac's. Elements are AIR, WATER, FIRE & EARTH.
Elements helps us to understand astrological signs and priniciple of Zodiac Signs. 12 Zodiac's are equally divided within 4 Elements.

Functions of the Elements:

Elements are basically Fixed, Movable or Mutable. Elements are very important to understand the functions of Zodiac Signs.


```
FIRE            - Movable or Cardinal
EARTH           - Fixed or Static
AIR/WATER  - Mutable or Common
```


<u>FIRE - Movable or Cardinal:</u>

Zodiac signs under this elements are very resourceful and out-going. They initiate, reasearch and make or change things happen. They take responsibility of the situations. They are good advicers and will not fit into subordinate positions. They think out of box and initiates new things into the life/job. Becomes overactive and restless for negative traits. This Zodiac is very supportive, silent and keeps their brains and actions going on. If you, distrub this zodaic, they become more fierce and you have to run to save your life.

<u>EARTH - Fixed or Static:</u>

This Zodiac's are determined, focused and presistence in thier life. Their mind will be focused on one thing at a time and work with will power till that particular thing gets completed. Very Firm and Stubborn in their attitude. Once the decision is done, they will not change their mind. They have a mode of resistance to change for negative traits, but will take long time for decision.

AIR/WATER - Mutable or Common:

This Zodiac is very felxible , changeable, adaptable and versatile. Their balance is between movable and fixed signs. They adapt themselves based on current needs and their surroundings. For negative traits, they are inconstant, vacillating, fluctuating and indecisive.

Zodiac Signs & Their Elements

1. ARIES -- MESHAM -- FIRE
2. TAURUS -- RISHABAM -- EARTH
3. GEMINI -- MITHUNAM -- AIR
4. CANCER -- KADAGAM -- WATER
5. LEO -- SIMHAM -- FIRE
6. VIRGO -- KAANI -- EARTH
7. LIBRA -- THULAM -- AIR
8. SCORPIO -- VIRUCHUGAM -- WATER
9. SAGITTARIUS -- DHANUSU --FIRE
10. CAPRICON -- MAGARAM -- EARTH
11. AQUARIUS -- KUMBAM -- AIR
12. PISCES -- MEENAM-- WATER

Astro House:

Four Elements are divided into 3 houses:

<u>First House or Main Pillars</u> of the Horoscope - Aries, Cancer, Libra

& Capricorn. Astrologically they are <u>Centric & Angles</u> of horo-scopes.

<u>Second House</u> to Angles are Materialized (<u>Money</u>) - Taurus, Leo, Scorpio and Aquarius

<u>Final House</u> after Angle & Material is Expenses - Gemini, Virgo and Pisces

In simple term, 3 houses can be seen as:
Birth -- Life -- Death (or)
Home -- Money -- Expenses (or)
Head -- Body -- Legs (or)
Mouth -- Stomach -- Exit

Houses can be further divided into 4 Spiritual Action or Dharma's Trinity.

Houses of Fire Signs:
Aries (Body), Leo (Heart) and Sagittarius (Higher Mind or Wealth).

Houses of Earth Signs:
Taurus (Possessions), Virgo (Comfort Life-Style) and Capcricorn (Fame, Relationship, kama & Honor).

Houses of Airy Signs:
Gemini (Sibilings), Libra (Marriage & Life-partner) and Aquarius (Close Associates, Friends, Liberation of final soul).

Houses of Water Signs:
Cancer (Envirement & Second half of the life), Scorpio (Death & regeneration), Pisces (Self undoing & Suffering).

PLANETS - COMPATABILITY

Lets check how the planets are playing the compatability levels with other planets. Compatability level means, that the planet can be either a Friend, an Enemy or Neutral.

The Sun
Friend: Moon, Mars, Jupiter
Neutral: Mercury
Enemy: Saturn, Venus

The Moon
Friend: Sun, Mercury
Neutral: Mars, Jupiter, Venus, Saturn
Enemy: Nil

The Mars
Friend: Sun, Moon, Jupiter
Neutral: Venus, Saturn
Enemy: Mercury

The Mercury
Friend: Sun, Venus
Neutral: Mars, Jupiter, Saturn
Enemy: Moon

The Jupiter
Friend: Sun, Moon, Mars
Neutral: Saturn
Enemy: Mercury

The Venus
Friend: Mercury, Saturn
Neutral: Mars, Jupiter

Enemy: Sun, Moon

The Saturn
Friend: Mercury, Venus
Neutral: Jupiter
Enemy: Sun, Moon, Mars

ASTRO STARS

There are totally 27 Stars, which are considered important in astrology.

These 27 stars are divided into Male and Female.
Male Stars are more of dynamic in nature &
Female Stars are more of passive ones in nature.

STARS & THEIR LOCATION

1. ASHWINI -- 00.00 Aries to 13.20 Aries
2. BHARANI -- 13.20 Aries to 26.40 Aries
3. KARTHIGAI -- 26.40 Aries to 10.00 Taurus
4. ROHINI -- 10.00 Taurus to 23.20 Taurus
5. MIRUGASHEERSHAM -- 23.20 Taurus to 06.40 Gemini
6. THIRUVAATHIRAI -- 06.40 Gemini to 20.00 Gemini

7. PUNARPOOSAM -- 20.00 Gemini to 03.20 Cancer
8. POOSAM -- 03.20 Cancer to 16.40 Cancer
9. AAYILAYAM -- 16.40 Cancer to 30.00 Cancer
10. MAGAM -- 00.00 Leo to 13.20 Leo
11. POORAM -- 13.20 Leo to 26.40 Leo
12. UTHIRAM -- 26.40 Leo to 10.00 Virgo
13. HASTHAM -- 10.00 Virgo to 23.20 Virgo
14. CHITHIRAI -- 23.20 Virgo to 06.40 Libra
15. SWAATHI -- 06.40 Libra to 20.00 Libra
16. VISHAGAM -- 20.00 Libra to 03.20 Scorpio
17. ANUSHAM -- 03.20 Scorpio to 16.00 Scorpio
18. KETTAI -- 16.40 Scorpio to 30.00 Scorpio
19. MOOLAM -- 0.00 to 13.20 Sagittarius
20. PURAADAM -- 13.20 to 26.40 Sagittarius
21. UTHIRAADAM -- 26.40 Sagittarius to 10.00 Capricorn
22. THIRUVONAM -- 10.00 Capricorn to 23.20 Capricorn
23. AVITTAM -- 23.20 Capricorn to 06.40 Aquarius
24. SADHAYAM -- 06.40 Aquarius to 20.00 Aquarius
25. PURATTADHI -- 20.00 Aquarius to 03.20 Pisces
26. UTHIRAATADHI -- 03.20 Pisces to 16.40 Pisces
27. REVATHI -- 16.40 Pisces to 30.00 Pisces

STARS & RULING PLANET

Every Star has been ruled by a planet. Lets see the name of the 27 stars and their ruling planets.

1. ASHWINI -- KETHU
2. BHARANI -- SUKIRAN
3. KARTHIGAI -- SURIYAN
4. ROHINI -- CHANDRAN
5. MIRUGASHEERSHAM -- SEVVAI
6. THIRUVAATHIRAI -- RAAGU
7. PUNARPOOSAM -- GURU
8. POOSAM -- SAANI
9. AAYILAYAM -- PUDHAN
10. MAGAM -- KETHU
11. POORAM -- SUKIRAN
12. UTHIRAM -- SURIYAN
13. HASTHAM -- CHANDRAN
14. CHITHIRAI -- SEVVAI
15. SWAATHI -- RAAGU
16. VISHAGAM -- GURU
17. ANUSHAM -- SAANI
18. KETTAI -- PUDHAN
19. MOOLAM -- KETHU
20. PURAADAM -- SUKIRAN
21. UTHIRAADAM -- SURIYAN
22. THIRUVONAM -- CHANDRAN
23. AVITTAM -- SEVVAI
24. SADHAYAM -- RAAGU
25. PURATTADHI -- GURU
26. UTHIRAATADHI -- SAANI
27. REVATHI -- PUDHAN

STARS & THEIR SYMBOL

Every Star has its own symbols to represent themselves.

1. ASHWINI -- HORSE'S HEAD
2. BHARANI -- YONI
3. KARTHIGAI -- RAZOR
4. ROHINI -- CHARIOT
5. MIRUGASHEERSHAM -- DEER'S HEAD
6. THIRUVAATHIRAI -- TEAR DROP'S
7. PUNARPOOSAM -- QUIVER
8. POOSAM -- UDDER
9. AAYILAYAM -- SERPENT
10. MAGAM -- THRONE
11. POORAM -- HAMMOCK

12. UTHIRAM -- FIG TREE
13. HASTHAM -- HAND
14. CHITHIRAI -- JEWEL
15. SWAATHI -- CORAL
16. VISHAGAM -- ARCH
17. ANUSHAM -- LOTUS
18. KETTAI -- AMULET
19. MOOLAM -- ROOTS
20. PURAADAM -- FAN
21. UTHIRAADAM -- TUSK
22. THIRUVONAM -- EAR
23. AVITTAM -- DRUM
24. SADHAYAM -- 1000 STARS
25. PURATTADHI -- FUNERAL COT
26. UTHIRAATADHI -- WATER SNAKE
27. REVATHI -- FISH

STARS & THEIR ENERGIES

Every Star's are divided into male and female animal energies. Male are dynamic and female are passive.

1. ASHWINI -- MALE HORSE
2. BHARANI -- MALE ELEPHANT
3. KARTHIGAI -- FEMALE SHEEP
4. ROHINI -- MALE SERPENT
5. MIRUGASHEERSHAM -- FEMALE SERPENT
6. THIRUVAATHIRAI -- FEMALE DOG
7. PUNARPOOSAM -- FEMALE CAT
8. POOSAM -- MALE SHEEP
9. AAYILAYAM -- MALE CAT
10. MAGAM -- MALE RAT
11. POORAM -- FEMALE RAT
12. UTHIRAM -- MALE COW
13. HASTHAM -- FEMALE BUFFALO
14. CHITHIRAI -- FEMALE RIGER
15. SWAATHI -- MALE BUFFALO
16. VISHAGAM -- MALE TIGER
17. ANUSHAM -- FEMALE HARE
18. KETTAI -- MALE HARE
19. MOOLAM -- MALE DOGS
20. PURAADAM -- MALE MONKEY
21. UTHIRAADAM -- MALE MANGOOSE
22. THIRUVONAM -- FEMALE MONKEY
23. AVITTAM -- FEMALE LION
24. SADHAYAM -- FEMALE HORSE
25. PURATTADHI -- MALE LION
26. UTHIRAATADHI -- FEMALE COW
27. REVATHI -- FEMALE ELEPHANT

STARS & GEM STONES

Every Star's have a gem stones, where the individual can wear for prosperity.

1. ASHWINI -- CAT'S EYE
2. BHARANI -- DIAMOND
3. KARTHIGAI -- RUBY
4. ROHINI -- PEARL
5. MIRUGASHEERSHAM -- CORAL
6. THIRUVAATHIRAI -- HESSONITE
7. PUNARPOOSAM -- TOPAZ

8. POOSAM -- SAPPHIRE
9. AAYILAYAM -- EMERALD
10. MAGAM -- CAT'S EYE
11. POORAM -- DIAMOND
12. UTHIRAM -- RUBY
13. HASTHAM -- PEARL
14. CHITHIRAI -- CORAL
15. SWAATHI -- HESSONITE
16. VISHAGAM -- TOPAZ
17. ANUSHAM -- SAPPHIRE
18. KETTAI -- EMERALD
19. MOOLAM -- CAT'S EYE
20. PURAADAM -- DIAMOND
21. UTHIRAADAM -- RUBY
22. THIRUVONAM -- PEARL
23. AVITTAM -- CORAL
24. SADHAYAM -- HESSONITE
25. PURATTADHI -- TOPAZ
26. UTHIRAATADHI -- SAPPHIRE
27. REVATHI -- EMERALD

STARS & NUMBERS

Every Star has a lucky number, on which the individual can plan to start or execute their plans.

1. ASHWINI -- 5, 7, 9
2. BHARANI -- 3, 6, 8
3. KARTHIGAI -- 1, 5, 7
4. ROHINI -- 2, 3, 9
5. MIRUGASHEERSHAM -- 3, 6, 9
6. THIRUVAATHIRAI -- 1, 4, 7
7. PUNARPOOSAM -- 2, 3, 9
8. POOSAM -- 5, 6, 8
9. AAYILAYAM -- 1, 5, 8
10. MAGAM -- 5, 7, 9
11. POORAM -- 3, 6, 8
12. UTHIRAM -- 1, 5, 7
13. HASTHAM -- 2, 3, 9
14. CHITHIRAI -- 3, 6, 9
15. SWAATHI -- 1, 4, 7
16. VISHAGAM -- 2, 3, 9
17. ANUSHAM -- 5, 6, 8
18. KETTAI -- 1, 5, 8
19. MOOLAM -- 5, 7, 9
20. PURAADAM -- 3, 6, 8
21. UTHIRAADAM -- 1, 5, 7
22. THIRUVONAM -- 2, 3, 9
23. AVITTAM -- 3, 6, 9
24. SADHAYAM -- 1, 4, 7
25. PURATTADHI -- 2, 3, 9

26. UTHIRAATADHI -- 5, 6, 8
27. REVATHI -- 1, 5, 8

STARS & COLOURS

Every Star has been represented by a colour, which is considered as lucky colour for the person born in that particular star.

1. ASHWINI -- RED/PINK
2. BHARANI -- WHITE
3. KARTHIGAI -- RED
4. ROHINI -- WHITE
5. MIRUGASHEERSHAM -- PINK
6. THIRUVAATHIRAI -- BLACK

7. PUNARPOOSAM -- YELLOW
8. POOSAM -- BLUE
9. AAYILAYAM -- GREEN
10. MAGAM -- RED/PINK
11. POORAM -- WHITE
12. UTHIRAM -- RED
13. HASTHAM -- WHITE
14. CHITHIRAI -- PINK
15. SWAATHI -- BLACK
16. VISHAGAM -- YELLOW
17. ANUSHAM -- BLUE
18. KETTAI -- GREEN
19. MOOLAM -- RED/PINK
20. PURAADAM -- WHITE
21. UTHIRAADAM -- RED
22. THIRUVONAM -- WHITE
23. AVITTAM -- PINK
24. SADHAYAM -- BLACK
25. PURATTADHI -- YELLOW
26. UTHIRAATADHI -- BLUE
27. REVATHI -- GREEN

STARS & NAMES

Names for the new born must start with the alphabet to get fortune in their life.

1. ASHWINI -- Chu, Che, Cho, La
2. BHARANI -- Lee, Lu, Lay, Lo
3. KARTHIGAI -- Aa, Ee, Oo, Ay
4. ROHINI -- O, Va, Vi, Vu
5. MIRUGASHEERSHAM -- Ve, Vo, Ka, Kee
6. THIRUVAATHIRAI -- Ku, Ghaa, Kha, Cha
7. PUNARPOOSAM -- Kay, Ko, Ha, Hee
8. POOSAM -- Hoo, He, Ho, Dah
9. AAYILAYAM -- Dee, Doo, Day, Doh
10. MAGAM -- Ma, Mi, Mu, Me
11. POORAM -- Mo, Ta, Tee, Too
12. UTHIRAM -- Tay, To, Pa, Pee
13. HASTHAM -- Pu, Sha, Nu, Tha
14. CHITHIRAI -- Pe, Po, Ra, Re
15. SWAATHI -- Ru, Re, Ro, Ta
16. VISHAGAM -- Ti, Tu, Te, To
17. ANUSHAM -- Na, Ni, Nu, Nay
18. KETTAI -- No, Ya, Yi, Yu
19. MOOLAM -- Ye, Yo, Bha, Bhe
20. PURAADAM -- Bu, Dah, Bha, Dha
21. UTHIRAADAM -- Be, Bo, Ja. Ji
22. THIRUVONAM -- Ju, Je, Jo, Gha
23. AVITTAM -- Ga, Gi, Gu, Ge
24. SADHAYAM -- Go, Sa, Si, Su

25. PURATTADHI -- Se, So, De, Di
26. UTHIRAATADHI -- Du, Tha, Jha, Na
27. REVATHI -- De, Tho, Cha, Chi

STARS & TREES

Every star has been associated with trees. This considered as a person's lucky tree and they can have it in their home garden.

1. ASHWINI -- ETTI TREE
2. BHARANI -- AMLA TREE
3. KARTHIGAI -- FIG TREE
4. ROHINI -- NAVAL TREE

5. MIRUGASHEERSHAM -- KARUNGALI TREE
6. THIRUVAATHIRAI -- THIPPILLI TREE
7. PUNARPOOSAM -- BAMBOO TREE
8. POOSAM -- PIPAL TREE
9. AAYILAYAM -- PUNNAI TREE
10. MAGAM -- BANYAN TREE
11. POORAM -- PARROT TREE
12. UTHIRAM -- ARALI TREE
13. HASTHAM -- NEEM TREE
14. CHITHIRAI -- VILVAM TREE
15. SWAATHI -- ARJUNA TREE
16. VISHAGAM -- WOOD APPLE TREE
17. ANUSHAM -- MAGIZHAM TREE
18. KETTAI -- BODH TREE
19. MOOLAM -- KUNTHIRIKKAM TREE
20. PURAADAM -- VANCHIKODI TREE
21. UTHIRAADAM -- JACK FRUIT TREE
22. THIRUVONAM -- ERUKKU TREE
23. AVITTAM -- DRUMSTICK TREE
24. SADHAYAM -- OAK TREE
25. PURATTADHI -- THEMBAVU TREE
26. UTHIRAATADHI -- KUDAPPANA TREE
27. REVATHI -- ILLUPPAI TREE

GOD & THEIR STARS

Like human being, every god has their birth star. That particular god's quality will resemble in the individual born in that star.

1. ASHWINI -- SHRI SARASWATHI DEVI
2. BHARANI -- SHRI DURGA DEVI
3. KARTHIGAI -- SHRI MURUGAN
4. ROHINI -- SHRI KRISHNAN
5. MIRUGASHEERSHAM -- SHRI CHANDRA SUDHESWARAN
6. THIRUVAATHIRAI -- SHRI SHIVA PERUMAN
7. PUNARPOOSAM -- SHRI RAMAR
8. POOSAM -- SHRI DHAKSHINAMURTHY
9. AAYILAYAM -- SHRI ADHISESHAN
10. MAGAM -- SHRI SURYA BHAGAWAN
11. POORAM -- SHRI ANDAL DEVI
12. UTHIRAM -- SHRI MAHALAKSHMI
13. HASTHAM -- SHRI GAYATRI DEVI
14. CHITHIRAI -- SHRI CHAKARATHAZHVAR
15. SWAATHI -- SHRI NARASHIMAN
16. VISHAGAM -- SHRI MURUGAN
17. ANUSHAM -- SHRI LAKSHMI NARAYANAR
18. KETTAI -- SHRI VARAZHI PERUMAL
19. MOOLAM -- SHRI HANUMAN
20. PURAADAM -- SHRI JAMBUKESWARAR
21. UTHIRAADAM -- SHRI VINAYAGAR
22. THIRUVONAM -- SHRI HAYAGRIVAR

23. AVITTAM -- SHRI ANANDA SAIANA PERUMAN
24. SADHAYAM -- SHRI MRITHUNJESWARAR
25. PURATTADHI -- SHRI EGAAMBARAR
26. UTHIRAATADHI -- SHRI MAHA ESWARAR
27. REVATHI -- SHRI ARANGANADHAR

CHARACTERISTICS OF STARS

Every star has its own character which is monitored and supported by its ruling planet.

1. ASHWINI - KETHU
Ashwini is the leading and first star in the Zodiac and governed

by Ashwin brothers (twin horses). This star is considered as reminder to the soul for their external element connections and main pillar of zodiac.

Person born in this star is very humble, serving others, contented family life and very truthful. Person is always active and busy doing something and keep themselves engaged. They love to keep others smiling and bring quick positive engergy to the surrounding. Person likes to keep home neat and keep decorating the home in traditional methods.

This person is very intelligent, vast learning and in fact an above-average person in knowledge. Ashwini is a carefree, happy, well developed brain power, connecting external souls, sacrifice, religious, silent thinker, philiosophical and straight ethical thinking. There is no place for negative thoughts or people. If anyone tries to approach or do any thing negative, then their life will become miserable by this star. They are very special, supported, blessed and well connected by all 9 planets to predict in advance and do remedies.

2. BHARANI -- SUKIRAN

Bharani is known as Restraint Star and ruled by Yama. The energy of Bharani is called as powerful, hot, harsh and fierce.s

Person born in this star is ungrateful, cruel, achieves notoriety, restless, fears water and wicked. Born as honest and will not change or modify their opinions to please others. They are fond of spreading rumors. They are very well business minded, magnetic personality, influential and fluctuating mood sets.

3. KARTHIGAI -- SURIYAN

Karthigai is known as born with nurture born power and governed by Agni Devan. This star burns evil and negative things. The

star rules battles, disputes and
war. Star denotes the capability of burning the negative and im-
pures the life to change in right path.

People born in this star can be critical, sarcastic and cutting wit.
They are aggressive, stubborn and short tempered. They have
very much filtered relationship with friends and relatives.

However this person would be fond of spicy food, academically
well done, gluttons, bright appearance, fond of opposite gender,
widespread fame and worried nature. They are self-motivated,
logical, vast learning, doubting mind, highly ambitious, creative,
hot bod, unsteady fortune, mechanical brains, enthusiastic and
brave character.

4. ROHINI -- CHANDRAN

Rohini is ruled by a creator, the Lord Bramha. People born in this
star have especially sexy and attrative eyes. Person born in this
star would be earning through agriculture, efficient in religious
activities, conversationlist, endowed with beauty, efficient, ge-
nius in arts and extremely materialistic.

This star will have control on their stubborn nature when leading
or working on groups. They would like to match their taste and
circle equally or above to their status. They do not give respect or
give a thought to the lower class people.

They are well educated, travel minded, spiritual, business
minded and have a magnetic touch in nature.

5. MIRUGASHEERSHAM -- SEVVAI

Mirugasheersha is governed by Lord Soma, the Moon. People
born in this star have a strong body and looking complexion.
They are basically outgoing in nature, so they search for beautiful
faces, places or will request girls in marriage.

They are sincere in their relationship, behaviour's with friends and relatives, expects vice-versa. Good grasping power, creative nature and learns quickly. They are sharp shooter and follows the virtual path. They always have personal and financial difficulties. For this star love marriage is best choice to enjoy and shine in their career. Likes research works, vast learner, leads high position, mystical are few traits of this star.

6. THIRUVAATHIRAI -- RAAGU

Thiruvaathirai is been monitored by Lord Rudra (Fierce form of Lord Shiva). Person born in this star stable minded, soft, afflicted by sickness, strong, earning by sacrifice, short-tempered and fear. They are very materialised and their work would be on foreign places or related to travel.

They behave very cool and during extreme situations and sort out the issues accordingly. Good Planners. The person thrifty, ungrateful, insincere, sinful and sometime spends foolishily.

They are open, flexible to change and often attempt to change their negative thoughts but ends in creating new negative thoughts. They hold responsible positions, religious, prone to litigation, brave, stress minded and artistic.

7. PUNARPOOSAM -- GURU

Punarpoosam is ruled by the lord Aditi (Mother Goddess). Person born in this star are very creative minded.
They keep renewing, restoring and returning their thoughts. Will not be able to take a stable decision.

This person will have oval face and good height. They start getting obese in mid of 30's. They tend to get into aruguments to win and show their intelligence. Creates disputes within families, Leads comfortable life but enjoying good health is a doubt.

This person has a numerous friends, practitioner of scriptures and sacred texts, possesses jewels, gems, ornaments and etc. They hava a spirit that can rise from ashes. They will be successful in almost all subjects except in business , contracts, deals or partnerships. They are nature minded, often faces success and failures, helping tendency, cultured and fluctuating thoughts.

8. POOSAM -- SAANI

Poosam is governed by the lord Brihaspathi (God of divine wisdom). This star basically denotes, replenish, preserve to protect, strengthen and multiply. Star increases good efforts, good karma, values spiritual and religious practices.

The person born in this star obeys their parents, regligious, healthy body, practices spiritual beliefs. The person has a good fortune, possesses good wealth, obey's law and believes that nobody should break the rules. They person would be basically tall and thin or short with oval face. They are very wealthy, devotional, soft nature, doubting, well places and jack of all trades.

9. AAYILAYAM -- PUDHAN

Aayilayam is been monitored by Lord Naga. The person is born wanderer, tavels unnecessarily, causes harm to others, wicked, sensualist, spends money on evil purposes. Has limited immunity against diseases. They become over-weight in their middle age.

They are associated actively with persons, services, organisation, where underground dealings are happening. Scope of entering politics is very favourable as they have good communication skills and they know how to win the opponents.

They are good administrators and have open views. They star is short tempered, moody, is wealthy, have harsh speech, slow in deeds and religious.

10. MAGAM -- KETHU

Magam is been governed by their Ancestors. Magam causes light and brightness. Star is very noble and straight forward character.

A person born in this star is strong hearted, respects parents, intelligent, learned and a winner of life. They respect elders and learn out of their experiences. They do not like to harm anyone unless if anybody harms them. They often fail, if do business independently, as making profit is not in their blood. Gives respects and expects the same.

They have commanding capacity, well devoted, wealthy, successful social workers and have fantastic artistic features. Women born in this star are real traits.

11. POORAM -- SUKIRAN

Pooram is been monitored by the Aryaman (God of unions & contracts). Star is the symbol of arts, beauty, creation, develops all levels with rest and relaxation.

Star is the symbol of luck and fortune. A person born in this star fosters many people, brave, lusty, rought, clever and cunning. Are generally handsome and have a long face. They hate underground dealings. Often feels difficult to handle the superiors and their confidence. Normally they are good eaters.

This person is very strong and cannot stand silent and see any illegal activities.

12. UTHIRAM -- SURIYAN
Uthiram is been monitored by Bhaga (Lord of Happiness).

A person born in this star is kind-hearted, charitable, achieves fame and possesses patience. They are straight forward and don't like to be taken as granted by situations or people. Those born in this star has good eye sight, strong physique and are generally ambitious. They have royal authority around them. They will have a happy and satisfied family life.

They follow and obey their parents and wife. They are approachable for monetary helps, sickness or for relief funds.

13. HASTHAM -- CHANDRAN
Hastham is governed by Savitar (Sun God). Star has the ability of achieving the goals with good manner. Their physical appearance will be thin and tall. Star respects Brahmins, elderly people, possesses wealth and well religious minded. They are diplomatic and suitable for any positions. Most people do not have graduation, but will be able to complete thirs tasks based on their experience.

Person is very creative and will do by their hands to give a personal touch. Good organizer and can manage the events in well planned manner. They do wonders in travel jobs. They are well wealthy, talented, influencer, sacrificing mind set, materialistic and little quarrelsome.

14. CHITHIRAI -- SEVVAI
Chithirai is been monitored Vishwakarma (Lord of cosmic craftsman). Star is considered as "Getting Opportunities or prosperity", world of delusions and maya, where the individual has to overcome. This star allows us to gain our positive karma brings from

the previous brith. It has a high spiritual effect and energy.

A person born in this star defeats thrir enemies instantly, extraordinary intelligent and expert in politics.
They are always in good health and will look younger than their actual age. The person born in this star has a powerful karma, they can predict and tell theirs and other's future.

Person will continuously pursue higher education in their life time, to keep updating their thirst for knowledge. They are mone minded, supersitious, magicians, hard minded and tactful.

15. SWAATHI -- RAAGU

Swaathi is governed by Vayu (Lord of Wind). This star is connectd with wind, breeze, air and akaash (Abode of Air). Swaati is much of destructive in stars. It is life-threatning unless we are aware of, how to remove the negativity created by this star.

A person born in this star is more material prosperity, is jolly and receives wealth from legal and illegal ways. They like to firt and keep flirting with opposite gender and keeps it in dark shadows even after getting married.

By nature, they are rude and would consider everybody including family members as slave to obey their orders. They would be thinking deep before taking any steps to make their mind and body balanced to bounce-back. They will go to any extreme, to make their things happen and will not be worried even if its injustice. They will be the sole reason to distroy their own marriage life. Even if they look good and soft natured, eventually they will be back with their original attitude.

Broad minded and attracts people easily. Cultured, submissive, learned, evil activites, underground contacts, wealthy and always want to be wealthy. They would like to be independent, aggressive and a real traitor.

16. VISHAGAM -- GURU

Vishagam is ruled by Agni and Indra (Lord of heat & light). Considered as "Star of Purpose". Star deals with greater long-term deals and not immediate returns.

A person born in this star is religious minded, performing rituals, unstable mind, unfriendly and unstable nature. Physically good looking, well-proportioned body, put on weight and become obese in their early ages. They would envy of others success. They lack on social networking, no much of friends, feel alone and isolated. They would feel the bitterness in their life. They will have happy married life and be good partners.

Star is jack of all and master of none. They speak and write well and excellent communicator. Very diplomatic and choice of word with sweet tongue. They are normally astrologer, brave, strong, admirer, dreamer and charitable.

17. ANUSHAM -- SAANI

Anusham is ruled by Mitra (Divine Friend). Anusham is a "Star of Success", balances both honouring in relationship and others. A person born in this star is enthusiastic, achieves fame, destroy the enemies, lustre, splendor, very creative, artistic and sensualist.

Some people have a peculiar characteristics.Will have an obstacle life, face several difficulties. They are successful only on foreign land and not in their home town. Good in organizational skills and has a healthy life style.

Normally they are not in good terms with their close relations and parents. High chances of political and social fields. They are well graduated, softness, devotional, royal positions, public speaker, musical talents and quickness.

18. KETTAI -- PUDHAN

Kettai is governed by Indra (Lord of the God's). The person born in this star is full of glamours, splendor, luster, achieves greatness and fames, brave, courage, power, glory, rich, excellent conversationalist and a hero. Anyone dealing with this star requires great effort and courage.

They have excellent physical apperance and good stamina. Fact is they are actually different from the qualities they appear. They are not clear in choosing their profession, life and frequently keep changing their jobs or business. They are expert in doing fashionable materials.

They are materialistic, love for ornaments, artistic, dreamers, agriculturist, love for costly dresses, brave, well-talented and philosophical.

19. MOOLAM -- KETHU

Moolam is ruled by Nirriti (God of Destruction). Considered as a very dangerous star next to Swaathi. Moola is a root, everything of basic nature is limited and finite.

Moolam does not indicates luck or fortune. The person born in this star is very materialistic, successful and leads a comfortable life. They are always interested in researching the root cause of any issues. They gain knowledge only through their hard work. They destruct their own family and marriage life.
They are peace loving people but will not give-up till what they want from others. They have multiple skills and keep changing their profession. No good relationship with their parents or siblings.

They spend money recklessly. They would love to keep counting their money every second, looks ambitious, wavering, doubt minded, illegal activites, talkative and travellers. Easily attracts the opposite gender, do not like to get committed, will cheat parents and others for their needs, cunning and will do anything for their They love to gain money without working.

20. PURAADAM -- SUKIRAN

Puraadam is governed by Varuna (God of Water). Star is known as "Invincible Star" and associated with war zones. Person born in this star is convincing, intelligent, empathize, influencer. They usually bring wealth, fame, wisdom and fertility.

They are very argumentive and try to prove their intelligence. Lack in logical reasoning, unstable decision-maker. Normally they like to do what they want and will not bother, consider or worry about others opinion. Good debaters and will win all aruguments. They are obstinate and will not accepts any demands or requests.

Determind in leading the groups, clever, selfish, brave, evil-minded, helpful, wealthy and deep thinkers.

21. UTHIRAADAM -- SURIYAN

Uthiraadam is ruled by Vishwadevas (Universal God). Star is also known as "Universal Star". Uthiraadam brings support, recognition, power not through the person effort but only through the support and alliances of friends or partners.

A person born in this star is workaholic, introspective, will become lazy when the task is not interested. They may not finish what they started. They are fair complexion with good health. They do not trust anyone that easily. Once the trust has been gained, they will support their circle of friends. But, not that easy to gain their trust.

Can be a good mediators in disputes, advisor, consultant, preachers, noble, wavering mind, basting, respected and very short-tempered. Need to be careful as the person might be opposite to you on disputes.

22. THIRUVONAM -- CHANDRAN

Thiruvonam is governed by Lord Vishnu (The Prevador). Star is known as "Star of Learning or Star of Listening). A person born in this star would always love to connect people together and direct them in a right direction.

A person born in this star will have many sons, well versed with scriptures, sacted texts, many friends and will destroy enemies. They will have huge network groups.

A person born in this star is helpful, respects others, faith on others, financially successful, leads luxuries life andtalkative. They will have slender body and medium height. Little rigid mind about their spouse and will not compromise while considering the qualities of Spouse.

They are normally adaptable, brave, wealthy, tactful, have evil company and good administrators.

23. AVITTAM -- SEVVAI

Avittam is monitored by the Vasus (God of Abundance) and known as "Star of Symphony".

A person in this star as an excellent attitude, behaviours, rich, practical, kind-hearted and powerful. They will be tall and lean with good resistance power to diseases. They look younger than their actual age. They are little short-tempered that might crush the opposite gender to any extreme. They have to take care of good health as they will not give importance till reaching the extreme stage.

More passionate about past and take time on learning it. Normally they have late marraige or unhappy in their married life. Parents must give the choice to this person to find a very much right partner to make their life happy and satisfactory. In many cases, this will result in love marriages.

They are patience, royal life, revengeful, suffering, social, brave and will have evil contacts.

24. SADHAYAM -- RAAGU

Sadhayam is ruled by Varuna (God of Water) and known as "Veiling Star". They deal human in mode of phyically and spritually.

A person born in this star is very cunning, clever, brave and destroys the enemies. They look like very simple, biased, god-fearing, religious, deals with spritiual and black magic activities. Normally thin and medium complexion. They always want to live a luxury life. They are cultured, writers, soft-hearted, religious and artistic.

Many people born and guided from roots lead a good and happy life with wisdom. Few would be a real traits. Female born in this star must have proper family guidance which will help them to settle peacefully. Very few woman goes on a wrong paths, tend to have physcial relationship with many men and maintain them parallely. They will not be easily satisfied when it comes to sexual life. Such Women will not have successful marriage and they will be in live-in relationship, so could be moved out if bored. They create sympathy with Men, to get easily brain washed and fall in addiction to such women.

If the negative side of this star is high, then they tend to do extreme black magic activities to get the things done and many a times destroys other family and friends life. Some might involve in prostitution, smuggling, contract killing and dangerous activities.

25. PURATTADHI -- GURU

Puratttadhi is governed by Ajai Kapada (One-Foot Serpent), known as "Star of Spiritual Aspiration". A person born in this star sacrifices a lot for a higher cause and try to makes difference.

They are very patience, mathematician, adaptable, intelligent has full control on themselves when being with right partners in life. They are normally slender, tall with charming personality and not risk takers. Destroys the enemies with logical methods and over thinking attitude.

They have a set of principles and will be followed at any situations.They are very kind and change accordingly to the situations to ensure not to hurt anyone. They spend money wisely and avoid misusing. Star is well-balanced and has helping hands only if convinced such as sympathy, generosity and kindness. Well practical minded with double face. Charity is not in their books.

A person born in star can easily gain confidence and respect from others even if financially weak. Gets married at right age. Their mental peace is more important. Must carefully select a life partner or will end-up due to spouse's attitude or will be too much disturbed. They are actualy spiritual, helpful, very patience, understanding not attached easily, boasting, energetic, quick thinker, little famous in friends circle and mini quarrelsome with loved ones.

26. UTHIRAATADHI -- SAANI

Uthiraatadhi is monitored by Ahirbudhnya (Depths of Atmosphere) and known as "Star of Warriors". A person born in this star follows virtuous path, famous, rich, believers on knowledge.

They will reachout to any extreme to help and are very merciful person. They will make fortune and earning in foreign land only or very far away from their home town. They will have a satisfactory and harmonious family life with children of joy and happiness.

Their behaviour is extremely praiseworthy, respectful and cordial. They look charming, scarifice their life for their loved ones, soft, devotional, helpful, religious, suspicious and a good planner.

27. REVATHI -- PUDHAN

Revathi is governed by Pushan (Sun God in norishing form) and known as "Star of Final Journey). Being the last star is also indicates the final journey of this human life.

A person born in this star controls his senses, amicable nature, sharp intelligence and aquires wealth. They are little short-tempered and difficult to make them accept our views. They have a set of principles, religious which they would follow and very much god-fearing. They have to depend themselves to progress their life.

Marriage life will be happy and their spouse would be more understanding. This person would normally graduate from overseas and will earn wealth there. It is difficult for him to survive in his home-town. They are little stubborn, authoritative and has required skills for the job. There is a high chance of becoming ambassador or representative of their country for political and cultural matters.

They are very noble, divine qualities, successful, artistic and well respected in society.

STAR EDUCATION & CAREER

Every Star's has its own speciality, where the person can shine in their education & career. Parents can plan their for their kids based on star speciality.

Every Star's has a specific temple and once in year visiting these temple will ensure happiness and remove obstacles in life. It is said that visiting on birth star is more auspicious.

1. ASHWINI:
Medical Surgeons, Druggists, Physiotherapist, Travel & Tourism, Agriculture, Healing Therapists, Botanical, marriage counselors, adventure sports, gynecologist, Stunts, Investigators, Goldsmith, Astrologyist & Authors.

2. BHARANI:
Gynecologist, Fertility Clinics, Morticians, Midwives, coffin makers, Maintaining Birth and Death records, Baby sitters, Teachers, Nannies, Children Toys, Chefs, Hoteliers, Caterers, Photographers, Models & Microbiologists.

3. KARTHIGAI:

Psychics, Teachers, Artisans, Astrologers, Gemstone Dealers, Critics, Managers, Building houses, Embroiderery, Ceramic Objects, Careers related with rehabilitation Centres.

4. ROHINI:

Costume and Ornament dealers, Cosmetics, Consultant, PRO, Architecture, Interior Designers, Textile Industry, Singers, Musicians.

5. MIRUGASHEERSHAM:

Scientist, Medicines, Medical Herbs, Linguists, Veterinarians, Linguists, Novelist, Poets, Writers, Fashion Designers, Advertising Agency, Real Estate Developers, Landscapers, Map Makers.

6. THIRUVAATHIRAI:

Non-ethical works, Thieves, Criminals, Science Fiction, Game designers, Researchers, Philosophers, Financiers, Investigators, Mystery solvers, Detectives, X-Ray specialist, Pschotherapists, Analysts & Mathematician.

7. PUNARPOOSAM:

Scholars, Scientist, Judge, Magistrates, Artistic, Writers, Film Visionaries, Travel & Tourism, Religious Jobs, Astronauts, Musicians, Psychologists.

8. POOSAM:

Priest, Minister, Politicians, Inventors, Scientists, Researchers, Consulers, Psychotherapists.

9. AAYILAYAM:

Manipulators, Pronography, Investigators, Prostitutes, Yoga Teachers, Hypnotists, Pschologist, Spirit Medium, Psychiatrists,

Tantrics, Cult Leaders, Spy & False Gurus.

10. MAGAM:
Businessmen, High Ranking, Self Dependent, Administrators, Super Achievers, Bureaucrats, Chairmen, Aristocrats, Architects, Gamers, Dramatists, Occultists, Astrologers, Archaeologists, Politicians & Genetic Engineering.

11. POORAM:
Fashion Designers, Fashion Product Dealers, Product Executives, production & Distribution of incenses, Jewelers, Silk Industry, Event Managers.

12. UTHIRAM:
Social Services, NGO's, Philanthropists, Marriage Consuelors, Teachers, Priests, Entertainment Industry, Astrologers, Professional Advisors.

13. HASTHAM:
Laborer, Artisian, Carpenters, Television Commentators, Magicians, Barbers, Physiotherapists, Bankers, Stock market dealers, Pickpockets, printing & publishing industry.

14. CHITHIRAI:
Builders, Real Estate, Architects, Interior Designers, Sculpture, Surgeons, Druggist, Singer, Mechanics, Landscapers, Graphic Artists, Production & Invention Machinery.

15. SWAATHI:
Business, Newreaders, IT industry, Skydivers, Educators, Trade-union, Diplomats, Socialites, Pilots, Aviation.

16. VISHAGAM:
Adventurers, National Security Services, Soldiers, Models, Radio

broadcasts, Professional Agitators, Immigration & Customs, Travel & Tourism Industry.

17. ANUSHAM:
Psychic & Hypnotists medium, Astrologers, Spy, Numerologists, Statisticians, Explorers, Mathematicians.

18. KETTAI:
Government Officials, Police, Army, Navy, Administrative positions, Unionist, Surgeons, Athletes, radar exerts, radio transmission activities.

19. MOOLAM:
Agriculture, Chefs, Physicians, Debaters, Aghoras, nuclear specialist, Entertainment industry, Financier, Black-Magicians, Illegal contacts, Public Speakers, Political Assistants, Investigators, Detectives and genetic industry

20. PURAADAM:
Shipping, Ice dealer, Marine experts, Navy, Fishing Industry, Weapon Experts, War Strategist, Shipping designers and Refineries.

21. UTHIRAADAM:
Magicians, Jugglers, Warriors, Wrestler, Actor, Organizer, Cricketers, Politician, Holistic Physicians and Elephant trainers.

22. THIRUVONAM:
Teacher, Linguists, PRO, Story tellers, Translators, News Broadcasters, Media, Show Hosts, Allopathy, Telephone Operators, Comedians, Scholars and Psychoanalysts.

23. AVITTAM -- CORAL

Jewellers, Grocers, Goldsmith, Traders, Musicians, Drummers, Orchestra bands, Song writers, Vocalists, Electronics, Metal dealers, Group Coordinators, Yoga and Healing profession.

24. SADHAYAM:

Medical representatives, Surgeons, Physicians, Herbalist, Drugs & Alcohol dealers and manfacturers, recycling industry, contract killers, smugglers, pimps and prostitutes.

25. PURATTADHI:

Undertakers, Diplomats, Jailors, Chefs, Coffin makers, Surgeons, Mystery solvers, perpetuators of dark technology, Researchers of AI, Extreme Ascetics, Homicide squads, Famous Aghoras, Mathematician and Hotelier

26. UTHIRAATADHI:

Sales Tax, Accountants, Auditors, Income-tax, Advocates, any job thats relates to Statistics and Accountancy.

27. REVATHI:

Dairy Farming, Aqucatic dealers, Poultry works, Butcher, Linguists, Road Planners, Construction, Foster homes, Illusionists, Hypnotists, Creative Artists, Entertainment Media and Conjurors.

STAR TEMPLES

Every Star's has a specific temple and once in year visiting these temple will ensure happiness and remove obstacles in life. It is said that visiting on birth star is more auspicious.

1. ASHWINI:
Piravi Marundeeswarar Temple - Thiruthuraipoondi
Dharbaranyeswarar temple - Thirunallar

2. BHARANI:
Agneeswarar Temple - Nallaadai
Vadaranyeswarar Temple - Thiruvalangadu

3. KARTHIGAI:
Gaathra Sundareswarar Temple - Kanjanagaram
Naganathar Temple - Nagapattinam

4. ROHINI:
Pandava Dhootha Perumal Temple - Kanchipuram
Sivayoginathar Temple - Thiruvisanallur

5. MIRUGASHEERSHAM:
Adi Narayana Temple - Enkan
Vana Durga Devi Temple - Kathiramangalam

6. THIRUVAATHIRAI:
Abhaya Varadeeswarar Temple - Adhiramapattinam
Agneeswarar Temple - Thirukollikkadu

7. PUNARPOOSAM:
Athitheeswarar Temple - Vaniyambadi
Abathsahayeswarar Temple - Alangudi

8. POOSAM:

Akshayapureeswarar Temple - Vilangulam
Karkadeswarar Temple - Thirunandudevankudi

9. AAYILAYAM:
Karkadeswarar Temple - Thirunandudevankudi
Subramanya Swamy Temple - Thirupurankundram

10. MAGAM:
Mahalingeswarar Temple - Thavasimadai
Thillai Kali Temple - Chidambaram

11. POORAM:
Hari Theertheswarar Temple - Thiruvarangulam
Sri Kalyanasundara Swamy Temple - Thirumanacheri

12. UTHIRAM:
Mangalyeswarar Temple - Edaiyathumangalam
Kucchiamman Temple - Poovalur

13. HASTHAM:
Kripakupareswarar Temple - Komal
Thyagarajaswamy Temple - Tiruvarur

14. CHITHIRAI:
Chittirairatha Vallabha Perumal Temple - Kuruvithurai
Thyagarajaswamy Temple - Tiruvarur

15. SWAATHI:
Prasanna Kundhalambika Temple, Tantreeswarar Temple - Sittukadu
Jambukeshwarar Temple - Thiruvanaikaval

16. VISHAGAM:
Kumaraswamy Temple - Thirumalai, Zenkottai
Pralayanathar Temple - Cholavandhan

17. ANUSHAM:
Lakhmsipureeswarar Temple - Thiruninriyur
Mahalingaswamy Temple - Thiruvidaimarudhur

18. KETTAI:
Pashupathinathar Temple / Varadaraja Temple - pasupathi temple, near kumbakonam
Angalaparameswari Amman Temple - Palladam

19. MOOLAM:
Singeeswarar Temple - Meppadu
Meenakshi Temple - Madurai

20. PURAADAM:
Akasapureeswarar Temple - Kaduveli
Bhakthajaneswarar Temple - Thirunavalur

21. UTHIRAADAM:
Brahma Pureeswarar Temple - Keezhapungudi
Dharmapuram Durga Temple - Mayavaram

22. THIRUVONAM:
Prasanna Venkatesa Perumal Temple - Thiruparkadal
Rajakaliamman Temple - Chetpet, Chennai

23. AVITTAM -- CORAL
Brahma Gnana Pureeswarar Temple - Korukkai
Magudeshwarar Temple - Kodumudi

24. SADHAYAM:
Agnipureeswarar Temple - Thirupugalur
Ardhanareeswarar Temple - Thiruhengode

25. PURATTADHI:
Thiruvaneswarar Temple - Ranganathapuram, Thirukattupalli
Adishesha Perumal Temple - Kanchipuram

26. UTHIRAATADHI:

Sahasra Lakshmeeswarar Temple - Theeyathur, Pudukottai
Panchanatheswarar Temple - Thiruvaiyaru

27. REVATHI:

Kailasanathar Temple - Karakudi
Pranavavyaghrapureeswarar Temple - Omampuliyur

STARS - MARRIAGE COMPATIBILITY

Compatibility in the marriage life is very important for both mental, physical and financial relation bonding. Matching should be made for the long life of male and for a successful marriage life.

Groom's Star should be more than 15 stars away from the Bride's Star. Less than 15 stars do not support long-life or marriage of groom.

Lets check-out how much strong affection seen in Zodiac Signs, towards each others in marraige life. In other words it is known Vasya Rasi

1. ARIES / MESHAM -- SIMHAM, VIRUCHUGAM
2. TAURUS / RISHABAM -- KADAGAM, THULAM
3. GEMINI / MITHUNAM -- KAANI
4. CANCER / KADAGAM -- VIRUCHUGAM, DHANUSU
5. LEO / SIMHAM -- THULAM
6. VIRGO / KAANI -- MITHUNAM, MEENAM
7. LIBRA -- THULAM -- KAANI, MAGARAM
8. SCORPIO -- VIRUCHUGAM -- KADAGAM
9. SAGITTARIUS / DHANUSU -- MEENAM
10. CAPRICON / MAGARAM -- MESHAM, KUMBAM
11. AQUARIUS / KUMBAM -- MESHAM
12. PISCES / MEENAM -- MAGARAM

Principles to drive the Couples:

Every Star is been represented in order of Brahmins, Kshatriya, Vaishya, Sudra, Anuloma and Pratiloma

If the women and men belongs to the same caste, check their match for its best, or else, men should belong to the higher caste comparing to women, except Anuloma and Pratiloma.

Anuloma and Pratilomas are allowed to marry each other and not in any other four castes. If, getting married with other castes, will always cause a trouble in marriage.

The main stars to be avoided in marriage life are Aayilayam,

Moolam, Swati and Sadhayam, as they are highly negative minded and destroy's the peace in marraige life.

Stars are arranged in an order for the easy community reference, in which community or star, the bride can be selected.

BRAHMIN:
Ashwini, Punarpoosam, Hastham, Moolam, Poorattathi.

KSHATRIYA:
Bharani, Poosam, Chithrai, Puraadam, Uthirattadhi

VAISHYA:
Karthigai, Aayilayam, Swaathi, Uthiraadam, Revathi

SUDRA:
Rohini, Magam, Vishagam, Thiruvonam

ANULOMA:
Mirugasheersham, Pooram, Anusham, Avittam

PRATILOMA:
Thiruvaathirai, Uthiram, Kettai, Sadhayam

Now lets check the attitude and characteristics to match the couples.
Characteristics are of 3 types and they are God, Human, Demon for each stars

STARS AS GOD:
ASHWINI, MIRUGASHEERSHAM, PUNARPOOSAM, POOSAM, HASTHAM, ANUSHAM, SWAATHI, THIRUVONAM, REVATHI

STARS AS HUMAN:

BHARANI, ROHINI, THIRUVAATHIRAI, POORAM, UTHIRAM, PURAADAM, UTHIRAADAM, PURATTADHI, UTHIRAATADHI

STARS AS DEMON:

KARTHIGAI, AAYILAYAM, MAGAM, CHITHIRAI, VISHAGAM, KETTAI, MOOLAM, AVITTAM, SADHAYAM

Favourable Matches:

GOD + GOD = FAVOURABLE
GOD + HUMAN = FAVOURABLE
GOD + DEMONS = UNFAVOURABLE
HUMAN + HUMAN = PARTIALLY FAVOURABLE
HUMAN + DEMONS = UNFAVOURABLE
DEMONS + DEMONS = FAVOURABLE

STAR HEALTH

Every person born in star will face an health issues. It is good to know the related diseases and change the food habits/life style's would help to have a healthy life.

1. ASHWINI:
Migrane, Severe Headache, Head Injury, Malaria, Brain Fever, Chicken Pox, Faint, Epilepsy.

2. BHARANI:
Eye Infection, Shivering Fever, Defective Eye Sight, Inflammation, Forehead Injury, Syphills, Dissipating Sexual Habits.

3. KARTHIGAI:
Fire Accidents, Back Head Injuries, Eye Infection.

4. ROHINI:
Breast Pain/Cancer, Sore Throat, Cold, Irregular Periods, Throat pain, Goiter.

5. MIRUGASHEERSHAM:
Inflamed Tonsils, Pimples, Adenoids, Venereal Distemper, Road Accidents, Fractures, Throat Pain, Constipation, Scitica.

6. THIRUVAATHIRAI:
Septic Throat, Asthma, Dry Cough, Mumps, Diphtheria

7. PUNARPOOSAM:
Bronchitis, Stomach Upset, Pneumonia, Tuberculosis, Dyspesia, Liver Trouble, Beriberi, Corrupt Blood, Thoraces.

8. POOSAM:
Tuberculosis, Nausea, Gall Stones, Cancer, Eczema, Hiccups, Ulcer, Jaundice.

9. AAYILAYAM:
Dropsy, Cold Stomach, Knees & Leg Pains, Indigestion, Windiness,

Breathing Toubles, Flatulence, AIDS, Phlegm.

10. MAGAM:
Sudden Heart Shocks, Backache, Food Poisoning, Fainting, Palpitation, Spinal Meningitis, Cholera, Kidney Stones.

11. POORAM:
Spine Curvature, Leg Pain, Blood Pressure, Swelling Ankles, Anemia, Affected Valves.

12. UTHIRAM:
Spotted Fever, Blood Pressure, Body Pains, Brain Blood Clotting, Sore Throat, Madness, Fainting, Bowel Tumors, Stomach Disorders.

13. HASTHAM:
Gastric Issues, Breathing Issues, Typhoid, Hysteria, Loose Bowels, Cholera, Diarrhea, Inferiority Complex, Shoulder & Arm Weakness, Dysentery.

14. CHITHIRAI:
Urinary Issues, Brain Fever, Renel Stones, Kidney Issues, Lumbago, Ulcers, Choleric Humour, Leg Pain, Worms, Itchingness, Appendicities, Sun Stroke, Headache, Brain Fever.

15. SWAATHI:
Leprosy, Gastric issues, Skin Issues, AIDS, Urinary Troubles, Corrupted Blood, Blood Infections, Polyuria Issues, Cancer, Eczema, Tumor, Urethra.

16. VISHAGAM:
Utreus Issues, Periods Issues, Tumor, Fibroid, Prostate Issues, Urinary Issues, Nose Bleeding, Dropsy, Reneal Stones, Rupture.

17. ANUSHAM:

Periods Issue, Sterlity, Fractures, Sore Throat, Constipation.

18. KETTAI:
Piles, Fistula, Tumors, Distemper in private parts, Arm Pain, Shoulder Pain, Leucorrhoea, Bowel Infection.

19. MOOLAM:
Pulmunory Issues, Rheumatism, Hip Diseases, AIDS, Stomach Upset, Corrupted Blood, Tumor, Liver Issues.

20. PURAADAM:
Rheumtism, Diabetes, Respiratory Issues, Corrupted Blood, Lung Cancer, Hip issues, Tumors.

21. UTHIRAADAM:
Skin Disease, Leprocy, Digestion Issues, Cardiac issues, Stomach Issues, Gastric Troubles, Exzema, Body Pains, Hear Palitation, Thrombosis.

22. THIRUVONAM:
Leprosy, Eczema, Pleurisy, Digestion Issue, Rheumatism, Tubeculosis, Filarial.

23. AVITTAM:
Malaria, High Fevers, Elephantiasis, Hiccups, Filarial, Pleurisy, Tumor.

24. SADHAYAM:
AIDS, Corrupted Blood, Urinary Infection, Leprosy, Blood Pressure, Rheumatic, Plapitration, Amputation, Fractures, Constipation, Insomnia.

25. PURATTADHI:
Ulcered Gums, Enlarged Liver, Jaundice, Hernia, Corns in Feet, Swelling Feet, Irregular Circulatory Issues, Intenstine Issues.

26. UTHIRAATADHI:

Dropsy, Cold Feet, Hernia, Foot Fracture, Tuberculosis, Constipation, Rheumatic Pains, Indigestion, Flatulence.

27. REVATHI:

Intestinal Ulcer, Deafness, Foot Deformities, Ear-pus, Gout in Feet, Abdominal Disorders, Crams.

Note: Listed dieseas are in general according to the stars, and cannot be directly validated on person's horoscope.
Eating Habits, Living Life-style also need to accounted.

DAMAGE/DEATH - PLANET

Every person in life faces damages and there is a certain point where the life span has an end.

It is not that everyone creates damage to our life. There are only few, who can create a collateral damages. In Sanskrit, it is known as "Pathaga Athipathi".

Pathaga Athipathi - Lord of Collateral Damage:

1. ARIES / MESHAM -- SATURN / SANI

2. TAURUS / RISHABAM -- SATURN / SANI

3. GEMINI / MITHUNAM -- GURU / JUPITER

4. CANCER / KADAGAM -- SUKIRAN / VENUS

5. LEO / SIMHAM -- SEVVAI / MARS

6. VIRGO / KAANI -- GURU / JUPITER

7. LIBRA / THULAM -- SURIYAN / SUN

8. SCORPIO / VIRUCHUGAM -- CHANDRAN / MOON

9. SAGITTARIUS / DHANUSU -- PUDHAN / MERCURY

10. CAPRICON / MAGARAM -- SEVVAI / MARS

11. AQUARIUS / KUMBAM -- SUKIRAN / VENUS

12. PISCES / MEENAM -- PUDHAN / MERCURY

Any person born in a planet has to exit the life at one point of time, and no one is allowed to stay/exist permanently in the planet.

Such like lord of colletral damage there is lord of death.
Certain planet / Zodiac has been given a task to end the person's life. In Sanskrit it is known as "Maraka Athipathi".

Maraka Athipathi - Lord of Death:

1. ARIES / MESHAM -- SUKIRAN / VENUS

2. TAURUS / RISHABAM -- CHANDRAN & GURU /MOON & JUPITER

3. GEMINI / MITHUNAM -- GURU & SEVVAI / JUPITER & MARS

4. CANCER / KADAGAM -- SURIYAN & SANI / SUN & SATURN

5. LEO / SIMHAM -- SUKIRAN & GURU / VENUS & JUPITER

6. VIRGO / KAANI -- GURU & / CHANDRAN JUPITER & MOON

7. LIBRA / THULAM -- SEVVAI / MARS

8. SCORPIO / VIRUCHUGAM -- SANI & PUDHAN / SATURN & MERCURY

9. SAGITTARIUS / DHANUSU -- PUDHAN & SUKIRAN /MERCURY & VENUS

10. CAPRICON / MAGARAM -- SANI & CHANDRAN / SATURN & MOON

11. AQUARIUS / KUMBAM -- SEVVAI & SUKIRAN / MARS & MERCURY

12. PISCES / MEENAM -- PUDHAN & SANI / MERCURY & SATURN

Share your feedback & Stories to padmam582@gmail.com

THANK YOU FOR READING

PADMA MANI